Staying Safe on Dates

There are issues of safety in every type of situation, including dating.

Staying Safe on Dates

DONNA CHAIET

THE ROSEN PUBLISHING GROUP, INC.
NEW YORK

Published in 1995 by The Rosen Publishing Group, Inc.
29 East 21st Street, New York, NY 10010

First Edition

Manufactured in the United States of America.

Library of Congress Cataloging-in-Publication Data

Chaiet, Donna.
     Staying safe on dates / Donna Chaiet. — 1st ed.
        p. cm. — (The get prepared library of violence prevention for young women)
     Includes bibliographical references and index.
     Summary: Uses real-life examples to illustrate how to handle various dating situations, including setting verbal and emotional boundaries for a relationship and dealing with sexual assault and rape.
  ISBN 0-8239-1862-9
     1. Young women—Crimes against—Prevention—Juvenile literature. 2. Violent crimes—Prevention—Juvenile literature.
3. Acquaintance rape—Prevention—Juvenile literature.
4. Relationship violence—Prevention—Juvenile literature.
[1. Teenage girls—Crimes against. 2. Acquaintance rape.
3. Crime prevention. 4. Self-defense. 5. Safety.] I. Title.
II. Series: Chaiet, Donna. Get prepared library of violence prevention for young women.
HV6250.4.W65C525   1995
613.6'0835'2—dc20   95-8475
                                                      CIP
                                                      AC

Contents

Introduction

Dating is a normal and healthy part of growing up, and most of us make it through our teen years with no more than a dented heart. The book focuses on how you can be more self-aware and take greater responsibility for those events and behaviors that are in your control. Staying safe on dates is more than avoiding "date rape" on a first date.

We address dating and personal safety in the larger context, not just in the worst-case scenario of rape. Dating means all the times when you are with someone (either alone or in a group) with whom you already have or want to have a romantic relation-

You may have to deal with some uncomfortable situations on dates, such as unwanted touching.

ship. Many of you will probably never have to deal with date rape. Virtually all of you, however, will have to deal with dating situations that make you uncomfortable and that you are not quite sure how to handle. You may be uncomfortable because of physical contact you are not ready for or because you are being verbally or emotionally abused. Personal safety means knowing how to take care of yourself in new or already existing relationships. It means being able to stop unwanted touching, hugging, or kissing. It means knowing how to

7

avoid verbally and emotionally abusive re-lationships as well as date rape.

Learning these personal safety skills is possible for everyone. Personal safety is not a list of dos and don'ts. Clearly, there are certain "rules" that it makes sense not to break. Most of you know that drinking alcohol or using drugs decreases your abil-ity to make good decisions. But even if you break a well-accepted safety rule, that does not give your date an excuse to touch you in a way you do not want, or to abuse you, or to force you to have sex. Likewise, hav-ing had one beer does not mean that you are "helpless."

Learning to stay safe on dates is not just about following certain rules. Even if you follow all the rules, you still may end up with a person who means you harm. Learn-ing personal safety skills means paying at-tention to internal cues about your feelings and knowing how to assess what is happen-ing and address the situation decisively.◆

chapter 1

Learn Your Boundaries

One of the foundations of personal safety is a concept called *boundaries*. A boundary can be defined as an emotional or physical line that marks or fixes a limit. Examples of physical boundaries are the fence around your schoolyard or the painted lines of a basketball court. A physical boundary can also be the space bubble that people maintain when they are with each other. For example, most of you probably talk to a friend with about one arm's distance between you. This is close enough to reach her shoulder but not close enough to hug without leaning toward each other.

This kind of physical boundary is also

We all have different boundaries. Some people are more comfortable with physical affection than others.

called a "comfort zone." The comfort zone is flexible. With people you know very well, it may be smaller than with a stranger. It can also change from day to day. If you have a cold, for example, you may not want to be close to anyone. If you feel sad, you may welcome a hug from a friend or parent.

In addition to physical boundaries, we also have emotional boundaries. An example of an emotional boundary is the way you prefer people to talk to you. Being yelled at for no reason is a violation of an emotional boundary, even though the person may be calling on the telephone.

Identify Your Boundaries

Understanding physical and emotional boundaries is a challenge. A good way to start is by examining your daily life. Look at your family. What kind of boundaries can you identify? Do your parents or caregivers hug and kiss you? When and under what circumstances? Do relatives hug you when you don't want to be hugged? How do family members talk to each other and interact? Can you voice your opinion? If so, on what topics is it okay for you to disagree?

Besides looking at your family, examine the culture that surrounds you. What kinds of boundaries can you identify in school? How do other teens interact? Is there a predominant religion in your community? If so, do you have the same beliefs?

Knowing as much as you can about your boundaries is one of your most important tools to stay safe on dates. Knowing how to identify what is and what is not okay behavior for you is the first step to maintaining personal safety. Let's look at some examples of behaviors.

Charlene and Ray

Charlene and Ray have been dating for two years. Ray has gotten into the habit of putting his hand on Charlene's knee when they are driving. Charlene does not like that; it feels as if Ray thinks he owns her. Instead of telling him to stop, Charlene gets silent (and angry). She doesn't understand why Ray doesn't "get it."

What are Charlene's options? Charlene is experiencing "unwanted touching." Simply put, anytime someone touches your body without your permission and it makes you uncomfortable, you are experiencing unwanted touching. This is a boundary violation. Even though you may like it when your boyfriend (or friends) touch you, Charlene does not. She is the one who sets her physical boundaries.

The problem is that Charlene has identified her boundaries, but she has not communicated this information to Ray. Ray cannot read her mind, even though we may think people should be able to—particularly people we know and care about.

Here is an option for Charlene. She can set a boundary with Ray by using some very simple language:

✓ **Step One**. Say what you are feeling. Begin the sentence with, "I feel . . ." and then fill in the blank. Charlene would say, "I feel uncomfortable . . ."

✓ **Step Two**. Say what makes you uncomfortable. The more specific you are, the better you communicate. Charlene would continue, "I feel uncomfortable when you touch my knee in the car."

✓ **Step Three**. Say what you want. This is important. Give the person a solution to the problem that is comfortable for you. "I feel uncomfortable when you touch my knee in the car. Please stop."

A nice guy stops. He does not want to make you uncomfortable. This kind of communication works because it gives Charlene an opportunity to own her feelings. First, she did not say, "Ray, *you* pervert, *you* make me feel . . ." This approach (using *you*) tends to put people on the defensive and make them less receptive to your message. Second, she identified the problem. She was exact. If she had said, "I don't like it when you touch my knee," it would not really have been accurate. It is not that Charlene *never* likes her knee being touched; it is just when they are driving. Finally, Charlene asked for what she wanted. "Please stop."

What if Ray did not take her seriously, or thought she was joking? Ray always drove

You are not responsible for someone else's feelings when you have set your boundaries.

with one hand on her knee, and Charlene had never complained before. He may be confused or hurt by her statement. First, Charlene is not responsible for what Ray feels. She spoke to him respectfully. She did not blame him or call him names. She told him how she was feeling. It is important to be true to our own feelings, not to take responsibility for other people's feelings, and to let people know when our boundaries have been crossed.

If Ray says, "You hurt my feelings," **15**

Charlene can reply that she did not mean to hurt his feelings. She still cares for him. She just wants him to stop a behavior. This is an important point. Charlene likes Ray. It is one particular behavior she wants to change. We can ask people to change behavior to respect our boundaries.

What if Ray says, "You must be kidding," and continues to keep his hand on her knee? Charlene needs to reset the boundary. She could simply repeat herself. Or she could gently move his hand and state the boundary like this, "Ray, I mean it. It makes me uncomfortable when you touch my knee in the car. Can we just hold hands instead?" If holding hands is an okay alternative for Charlene, that is a great solution. It still gives Ray the feeling of being connected but in a way that makes Charlene more comfortable.

Daffney and Ryan

Daffney and Ryan started going out six months ago. Ryan is very outgoing and has the highest grades in their class. Daffney is quiet and shy. She has only been in the

United States for four years. She speaks English fluently but with an accent. Daffney believes that she is not as smart as Ryan because she doesn't get straight A's. A couple of weeks into their dating, Ryan started to correct her pronunciation of certain words. He did this in public, and sometimes people would laugh. In addition, Ryan also implied that Daffney was probably not as smart as he because she was not educated in the United States all her life and doesn't get straight A's. He used to be more considerate of her feelings. What is happening and what can Daffney do about it?

Daffney is experiencing emotional abuse. Even though it is isolated and occurs in limited situations, Ryan's behavior is abusive emotionally. You may think that Daffney is too sensitive and should lighten up. Ryan treats her well in every other respect; what is the problem? The problem is that for Daffney the public corrections and the subtle implications about her educational background cross her emotional

When someone crosses your physical or emotional boundaries, you have the right to tell them so.

boundaries, and she feels belittled. Ryan's conduct might not bother another girl. She might like the attention and be confident that grades are just one indication of a person's intelligence. The issue is that Daffney feels put down by Ryan's comments.

Ryan's conduct is crossing Daffney's emotional comfort zone. His comments are not okay with her. The solution to her problem is similar to Charlene's.

✓ **Step One**. Identify your feelings and state them, beginning with "I." Daffney could say, "I feel hurt..."

✓ **Step Two**. Identify the behavior spe-
cifically. "I feel hurt when you correct
my speech in public."

✓ **Step Three**. Ask for what you
want. "Please do not do it publicly
anymore."

Ryan may not know that there is a problem. He may believe that Daffney likes the
attention or that she would rather be corrected than continue to mispronounce
words. It would probably help if Daffney
could tell him that it is not so much being
corrected as being corrected in public that
embarrasses her.

What about his implications regarding
her intelligence? This is a tricky situation,
because he doesn't come right out and say,
"You are so stupid." That kind of comment
is easily understood, if uncalled for. But
Daffney perceives that Ryan is subtly
putting her down because of her foreign
education and failure to make straight A's.
Ryan needs to realize that grades are just
one measure of intelligence. Even though
Ryan is an outgoing guy, he is probably
insecure. He doesn't sound like a mean or

It can be difficult to let your date know how you feel about his
behavior.

nasty person, and the rest of his behavior proves that.

Daffney's goal is to get Ryan to change his behavior even though she may not be able to change his mind about foreign education and grades.

Let's start at the beginning. Say what you are feeling, identify the problem, and ask for what you want. Daffney would continue, "Ryan, I also feel put down when you imply that my education is not as good as yours and that you are smarter than I am. Can we talk about this?" It would probably be best for Daffney to open a discussion on the topic, rather than just asking him to stop. Ryan may not be aware of his behavior. The way to educate people we care about is to have two-way discussions. The goal is to identify the issue so that we can create a way to stop the behavior.◆

chapter 2

Dating Violence

You may be thinking that this is all well and good when the behavior is not violent. If someone is hitting you, "I feel . . . please stop," is just not going to do it. You may be right. In more extreme examples of boundary violations, which include physical violence, it may not work to ask the person politely to stop.

Alice and Ted

Alice and Ted have been going out for almost a year. During the course of their relationship, Ted's parents split up. At that time Ted became angry and short-tempered. He began to push Alice around, and on one occasion he slapped her. Alice

People do not have the right to abuse others physically.

really cares for Ted and knows he is going through a tough time. She feels that if she can ride out the crisis, Ted's behavior will stop.

What is happening? Alice is in a physically abusive relationship. Regardless of Ted's problems, resorting to physical force is not okay. It doesn't matter that Ted's actions left no marks or scars. You don't need a broken arm or bruises to identify the relationship as physically abusive.

What are Alice's options? It is important **23**

Hotlines and rape crisis centers are good sources of information and other resources for women suffering from abuse.

that she set a firm and clear boundary and be willing to enforce it. She could say, "Stop pushing me around. I want to help you, but if you don't stop I will end the relationship." Alice, of course, has to be ready to carry through. More likely than not, Ted's behavior will not get better without the help of a professional.

The only way for Alice to ensure her safety is to leave the relationship and avoid Ted. That is bitter medicine, but the goal is to learn to stay safe. Preparing yourself to leave a relationship is hard, but many girls have done it. Get help from supportive friends and family who will not blame you for staying in the relationship as long as you did. Seek help from a professional such as your guidance counselor, or call a rape crisis center. Even though you have not been raped, the center will know of resources in your community to help you. Encourage your boyfriend also to seek the help of family, friends, and professionals. If he is willing to admit that he has a problem, he may well be able to accept help.◆

chapter 3

Date/ Acquaintance Rape

In the past few years concern has been growing about date rape and acquaintance rape. Date rape is defined as forced sexual intercourse or other sexual act between a dating couple or while on a date. Acquaintance rape is the same but between two people who know each other but are not dating. Controversy also has been growing over the extent of the problem. Our intent is not to debate the number of women who experience this crime (statistics vary, but between two thirds and three quarters of women surveyed reported that they had been raped by someone they knew), but to address what we can do

Any time one person forces another to have sex—even if they've had sex in the past—it is rape.

about it if we confront it. Let's look at two other scenarios with Ted and Alice.

Revisiting Alice and Ted

Alice and Ted continued to date, notwith-standing her concern that Ted was becoming more violent. One evening they were kissing and necking. They had had sexual intercourse on other occasions, but this time Alice wanted to stop and she said so. Ted told her that he knew she wanted it and pinned her arms above her head. Alice   **27** *tried to get free, but couldn't. He forced her to have sex with him against her wishes.*

In this situation, Alice was a victim of date rape. Even though they had been sexually active before he forced her, it is still rape. Consent on numerous previous occasions does not mean consent forever. Each time people have sexual relations they must give mutual consent; otherwise it is forced sex. Forced sex is rape.

What if Ted forced Alice to have sex on their second date, but he did not use violence? Instead, he drove her into the woods one winter evening and said that if she did not have sex with him he would leave her there. She had no idea where she was and was afraid she would not survive the night because it was so cold. Alice "agreed" to have sex. Did she consent to sex?

The answer is no. Under those circumstances, Alice was raped because she was coerced into having sex. Had she not complied, she feared she might not survive the night alone in the woods. Physical violence is not the only test of rape. If a woman is coerced or blackmailed or so drunk that she does not know what is going on, and her date forces her to have sex, that is rape.

Looking for Reasons

You may be thinking, "How does this happen?" Why would your boyfriend hit you or force you to have sex? Why would a guy coerce or blackmail you into sex?

Those questions are complex and no one has the complete answer. Some social scientists believe that the media have a lot to do with the problem. Violence on television and in the movies is rampant. Some people believe that constant exposure to violence desensitizes people to it. Violence becomes an acceptable, if not actually desirable, behavior. Using violence as a way to solve problems and get what you want becomes commonplace.

Others believe it is the way the media link violence to sex. Advertising is notorious for this. Photographs show women's body parts separate from the rest of the

Some people believe that pornography degrades women.

body; for example, a panty-hose ad that shows only a woman's legs. This is sometimes called dismemberment. People argue that this type of advertising encourages people to view women as body parts rather than as people, and it is an unhealthy (and unrealistic) way of looking at women.

Similarly, some people hold that pornography hurts women by setting standards for what is considered beautiful and sexy, even if it is degrading. In magazines like *Playboy*, this generally means a naked woman with very large breasts. In more graphic magazines, it may mean a woman tied to a bed or a woman who is carrying a whip or being whipped. This kind of representation objectifies women and gives men a false picture of women and what they want sexually.

Others believe it has to do with traditional myths about men and women:

✓ Women want sex but say no.
✓ No means yes.
✓ If a guy pays for a date, he has "bought" the girl for the evening and is entitled to have sex.

✓ Guys can't control themselves sexually.
✓ Once a guy is aroused, he cannot stop.

That list of myths could go on and on. The truth is that no means no. If a man pays for a date, all he is entitled to is a thank you. Guys can control themselves sexually. They can stop even if they have an erection.

We could spend years debating why violence is prevalent in our society or why men force or coerce women into sex. However, it is equally, if not more, important to discuss what we can do as a response to violence in our own lives. We may not be able to control the content of television, or what magazines our boyfriend reads, but we can and do have control over our reactions and behavior. We accept the fact that some men believe that the price of a dinner entitles them to sex. Some men believe that violence is an appropriate method of solving personal problems. Once we accept these realities, we can make choices about our behavior.◆

chapter 4

Societal Conditioning

Learning how to respond to the possibility of interpersonal violence means examining how we have been socialized and what media messages we believe about ourselves as females.

Women have been socialized to be passive and quiet. "Be a good girl." This often means putting other people's needs above your own. How often have you let relatives give you a hug or a kiss, even though you did not want it, to avoid hurting their feelings? This kind of behavior is so deeply ingrained in most of us that we are barely aware of it. Not respecting our own feelings implies somehow that what we want or feel **33**

You do not have to allow someone to touch you if you don't want them to.

is insignificant. Additionally, it implies that it is okay for someone to touch us even if we don't want it. We therefore conclude that we do not own our bodies and do not control who touches us.

Moreover, women are not encouraged to be physically active (although this may be changing). Women are not given as many opportunities to play physical sports, particularly contact sports. They therefore miss at least one experience of getting in touch with their bodies. Women are not given the message that they are physically strong and can withstand physical wear and tear. Female athletes learn that they can compete even with a sprained ankle or wrist. Most women have never experienced that kind of challenge.

Taken together, societal conditioning diminishes our ability to have our feelings respected and to have a satisfactory relationship with our bodies. This hinders us from taking care of ourselves in interpersonal relationships. What are your options? As mentioned earlier, knowing your physical and emotional boundaries is the foundation of personal safety. Here are some exercises to help you identify where you stand.

Checking Your Boundaries

See if you notice a difference in the space you leave between you and a friend or teacher as compared to a salesperson whom you do not know. When someone moves into your personal space, try to adjust your body so that you have more room. If you can't move, ask the person to take a step back. Notice how close you let strangers get to you when you are riding public transportation or shopping in the mall. See how many people touch you without asking permission in any given week. This includes friends and family members. If it is too many, try to persuade them to ask permission before they hug or touch you. Notice whether you hug or touch people without asking permission. See if there is any correlation between the two situations.

Similarly, see if you are aware when someone crosses an emotional boundary. This is a little trickier than physical bounda-

Try to be aware of what your body language is telling those around you.

ries, but it is equally important. People may cross your boundaries in small ways. For example, do people borrow money from you and not pay it back? Is that okay? If not, ask for your money back or stop lending it. Learn to say no when people ask favors that you do not want to do. Are you the one who always goes where your friend wants to go or never gets to see the movie you want to see? These are all examples of emotional boundary violations. To prevent them, check up on your feelings and emotions. Do you feel taken advantage of? Do you feel that you never get your way? Do you always make the concessions? Obviously, it is good to compromise; just be sure it is evenly balanced in any relationship.

Besides monitoring your boundaries, begin to notice your body language, eye contact, and facial expressions. These are critical in maintaining personal safety. Pay attention to your body language when you set a verbal boundary. Do your shoulders slump forward? Do you rock back and forth? Do you look at the ground? This type of body language may not match what you are asking for verbally.

The way we carry ourselves says more about us than we may imagine. Street criminals are expert at selecting people as targets based on their body language. They can tell who is likely to be an easy mark. It is possible that the way we feel about ourselves ("I'm fat; ugly; stupid; worthless") is expressed in our body language. Boyfriends or potential boyfriends pick up on these nonverbal cues and get a sense of your feelings of self-worth. They can then capitalize on this and push your boundaries.

Pay attention to your own body language. If it is not saying what you want it to say about you, change it. Remember to keep your shoulders and head up and back. Walk in a confident manner. Don't rock back and forth when you are standing still. Take up a lot of space with your body, even if you are petite. That might mean putting your hands on your hips rather than folding them on your chest.

The same thing can be said about eye

contact and facial expressions. Girls are socialized that it is impolite to stare, and that we should smile to get what we want. Making eye contact with someone is a great way to say, "I see you, and you cannot ignore me." Notice whether you look away from someone when you are uncomfortable. What does that say about you? Notice how often you smile when you are not really happy. Do you smile or even laugh when you are scared or uncomfortable? What does it say about you if you turn your eyes away and smile when a boyfriend corrects your accent in public? What if Daffney had stared at Ryan and gotten teary-eyed when he made his public corrections? It would have been hard for Ryan to believe that she liked his behavior. What if Daffney's eye contact, facial expression, and body language had just ignored it?

To get the best results and maintain the highest level of personal safety, it is crucial that the way we look, sound, and behave communicate the same thing.◆

chapter 5

Prevention: Verbal and Physical Self-Defense

To get the most out of verbal boundary-setting, it is important to understand some other concepts about personal safety. We have addressed societal conditioning and how traditional notions of female conduct can inhibit our ability to stay safe. Being quiet and passive are considered feminine traits. Being silent in a relationship makes it very difficult to get what you want and to stay safe.

Practice asking for what you want in less emotionally charged situations. For example, if your friend brings two different sandwiches for lunch and asks which one you want, ask for the one you want, not the one

Practice asking for what you want. If you are served the wrong dish at a restaurant, ask that the mistake be corrected.

you think she wants you to have. If she asks, answer honestly. If a waiter brings you the wrong order for dinner, send it back. You don't have to accept a meal you didn't order and don't want. If a teacher makes a sexist or racist comment in class, say something. Learning how to break the silence is an important part of learning how to stay safe.

Denial

42   Along with this concept goes avoiding

denial. Denial is a psychological term for the way some people cope with the world. It is a dangerous coping mechanism when used with personal safety. For example, a girl continues to date a guy who is violent by telling herself, "There's no problem."

Rationalization is another dangerous coping mechanism. The same girl might rationalize her situation by saying, "He hits me because he cares." If we pretend that no problem exists or lie to ourselves about the problem, it becomes harder for us to stay safe.

Earlier we talked about the fact that some men have certain beliefs about dating behavior. Even though we would love to live in a world without violence where everyone treats others respectfully, we know better. All we have to do is read the papers, listen to the news, or hear friends talk about their experiences. In order to be able to take care of yourself, you must first accept the fact that there is a problem and behave accordingly. Do not deny the problem or rationalize it. Confront it.

Let's look at a situation in which a teen-ager's safety is being compromised. Try to identify the choices that Lin makes. What would you do in her situation?

Lin

Lin is at a party. Her ride is drunk, and Lin does not have enough money to take a cab home. The guy she has been talking to offers her a ride home. Lin feels pretty good. She is a little light-headed, although she has had only one beer. The guy seems sober enough to drive and acts like a nice guy.

What choices is Lin making? First, she is examining the situation carefully. She does not just say okay. She checks her internal cues about the guy and the situation. She has had one drink, he appears sober, he seems "nice." However, we all know that she is taking a risk. He is a virtual stranger. They both have had alcohol.

What is important is that Lin is staying alert and taking inventory. What could she do before she actually leaves the party with this guy? She could ask other people if he is okay and maybe get a little more objective information about him. She might also tell the people staying at the party that she is leaving with him and that if she doesn't call from home within 20 minutes they should notify the police. She might even say this within earshot of the guy; it demonstrates a good level of awareness.

What if they get in the car and the guy puts on a romantic CD and says, "Is it okay if we stop at my friend's house before I take you home? He's having a private party. We could have another drink."

Instant alarms should be going off in Lin's head. He is obviously misinterpreting her accepting a ride home as continuing their time together. This is the time to set a clear boundary. "No. But thanks, anyway. My parents are expecting me in 20 minutes." If Lin says this, looks down, shrugs, and smiles a little, that does not communicate a clear message. Lin should say no verbally as well as with her body language, eye contact, and facial expression.

What if he says, "I need to stop by a

friend's house and pick up a sweater I left earlier. Is that okay?" Lin can say, "No. I really need to get home as soon as possible. My parents are expecting me." But what if she says okay? They go to his friend's house and find a few couples, obviously drunk and stoned. He heads off to get them drinks.

The bells should be going off in Lin's head again. This is not a safe situation. She should leave immediately even if it means walking a long way home or calling her parents to pick her up. Lin needs to be constantly reassessing the situation as it relates to her personal safety.

What if they get in the car and he starts driving in the wrong direction? Should Lin assume he knows where he is going? No. She should ask, "Where are you going? I live north of here, not south." What if he says, "I thought we could stop by at a friend's house." Time for a clear verbal boundary.

What if they get in the car, he starts driving in the wrong direction, and Lin is not really paying attention? After a couple of miles he parks in an empty lot, turns on some music, and leans over to kiss her. This is the time for a clear verbal boundary. "I do not want to kiss you. Stop." What if he continues? Lin should repeat herself, checking her body language and facial expression. Making clear eye contact, she should put up a hand between them like a stop sign, saying, "STOP—I mean it!" loudly and clearly.

What if he continues? Lin has to assess her situation and realize that it is dangerous. "I have set a clear verbal boundary; it is not being respected. Someone is trying to touch my body and kiss me. I am in danger of date rape." A number of people believe that being passive in the face of rape is the best way to survive without injury. New studies indicate, however, that physical resistance, including loud verbal responses, is the best way to avoid being raped. An article entitled "The Effects of Resistance Strategies on Rape" (*American Journal of Public Health,* November, 1993) reported that forceful verbal resistance, physical resis-

The telephone is just one place you can go for help. Stores, gas stations, and ringing someone's doorbell are a few others.

tance, and flight are all associated with rape avoidance.

Your Options

Here are your options:

✓ Yell very loudly.
✓ Honk the horn.
✓ Get out of the car, particularly if you believe you can get to a telephone and call for help.
✓ Thrust your handbag or another object into his throat.
✓ Reach for his groin area and try to grab and squeeze the testicles.
✓ Be passive.

Any situation has numerous variables. Are you in a car, lying on a beach, in a deserted place, close to people, at home, in his home? Do you have any self-defense training? There is no one right way to resist date rape. Remember, if you choose a physical response, go 100 percent. Do not apologize. Do not try to protect him. Hit hard to target areas (eyes, throat, temple,

The best way to learn self-defense skills is to practice them in a
self-defense class such as Prepare Self-Defense.

groin, and shins), and be ruthless. Use your anger and indignation at what he is trying to do to make you ruthless. There are no rules in a fight; go for it.

Self-Defense

The best way to learn effective physical self-defense is to practice it. In the "Get Prepared" workshops that my organization, Prepare, teaches to teen girls, the students learn techniques by practicing them on a padded attacker. The padding enables the students to use techniques to the most vulnerable parts of a man's anatomy, including his eyes, throat, nose, and testicles. The situations are dynamic and changing, which forces the student to think on her feet. Some of the scenarios start with the girl lying down, which is frequently where you find yourself in a rape situation.

Another advantage of training in these realistic scenarios is that the students experience the adrenalized state. The fight or flight syndrome is a natural response for humans (and animals) when confronted with fear or danger. In this adrenalized state, our bodies are preparing to run or fight in order to survive. Students also practice how to deal with the freeze response, another biological response to fear or danger. In this situation the body shuts down or freezes, unable to do anything. By practicing, and yelling, and becoming confident in technique, the students shorten the freeze response so that they can move to the fight/flight syndrome, which can make the person powerful, fast, and stronger than she ever thought she was.

Remember that even women who had had no self-defense or martial training have successfully defended themselves. Fighting spirit is more important than fighting technique. Fighting spirit is the instinct that says, "My life is worth fighting for. No one has the right to hit me or rape me, and I will do whatever I need to do to stop it."◆

chapter 6

More Safety

So far we have discussed maintaining personal safety by keeping yourself out of physical danger and out of emotionally or verbally abusive situations. This chapter discusses safety from sexually transmitted diseases and from AIDS.

The decision to have sexual relations with a boyfriend is important. Your family values, religious upbringing, and culture greatly influence your behavior. The best way to avoid sexually transmitted diseases including AIDS (which is lethal) is to abstain from sexual intercourse or the exchange of body fluids—blood, semen, and vaginal secretions.

If you are considering beginning a sexual **53**

relationship, give it serious thought. Examine all the ramifications of the choice. Do not engage in denial by pretending that the decision does not exist and waiting until you and your boyfriend are already kissing. That is no time to make a clear-headed decision.

Sexual Boundaries

As in maintaining personal safety, know your sexual boundaries and don't be afraid to state them. You might say to your boyfriend, "It is okay to touch my body, but only above the waist." That is a clear boundary. Setting boundaries like this so that your physical relationship proceeds in a respectful and cautious manner is good personal safety. It ensures that no more happens than you have planned for and want.

What if you decide that you are ready for sexual intercourse? Set a boundary about using condoms well in advance. This is one of the only rules that cannot be broken. If you are going to engage in adult behavior, you must make adult choices. Using condoms with nonoxynol-9 as a lubricant is the

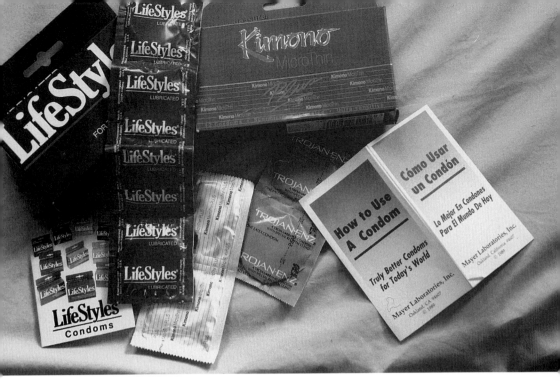

Using condoms is essential if you choose to have sex.

best way to avoid sexually transmitted diseases and AIDS. Remember that condoms are not 100 percent perfect, and you are still taking a risk. There is no such thing as safe sex, only safer sex. Make sure that you and your boyfriend know how to use a condom properly. Read the literature, talk to your sex education teacher, your parents, or other trusted adults. Talking with an older sibling might be helpful, but remember that she may not know much more than you do.

Trust your instincts. If you have doubts about having sex, for any reason whatever, don't.◆

Conclusion

This book began by stating that personal safety is more than a list of "dos and don'ts." However, there are some general guidelines that should help to keep you safe in most situations. Begin by learning your physical and emotional boundaries. Identify them, and practice enforcing them. The more you practice on the smaller things in your life, the easier it becomes when the stakes are high. Learn to pay attention to your inner voice. If something feels wrong, then it is wrong. Address the problem quickly and decisively. Problems become worse when they are left alone.

Be careful about the situations in which

you put yourself. Be prepared for as many different problems as possible. Carry money so that you have a way to get home. Do not isolate yourself from friends at a party. Don't add to your vulnerability by using alcohol or drugs. If you go somewhere, let people know where you are going and when you should be back. Don't be afraid to make a scene. Study self-defense and martial arts.

If you find yourself in a dangerous situation, assess the variables, figure out what you have control over and what your choices are. If you choose to make a physical response, be ruthless. If you are physically passive, realize that what happens to you can still be called rape even though you were not beaten or physically threatened; you did not do anything wrong. Get help as soon as possible. Call 911 or a local rape crisis center.♦

Glossary

acquaintance rape Forced sexual intercourse (or other sexual act) between two people who know each other.

adrenalized state See fight/flight syndrome.

body language The way we hold our body and the messages and information that communicates to others.

boundary The physical or emotional distance with which a person surrounds herself. Emotional limit.

boundary violation A person's invading your comfort zone with physical touching, verbal intimidation, or disregard for your feelings.

comfort zone Your own personal physical boundary.

date rape Forced sexual intercourse (or other sexual act) between a dating couple or while on a date.

denial Psychological coping mechanism in which you pretend or believe that what is happening is not happening.

directive language Words that clearly state what you want: "Stop," "Go away," "Leave me alone," "Back off."

dismemberment Term used to describe the way women are portrayed in advertising and media as parts of bodies rather than as whole human beings.

fight/flight syndrome Biological response in which adrenaline and other hormones are released into the bloodstream, enabling a person to fight or run away.

freeze response Biological response to fear or danger that can paralyze a person.

internal cues One's own thoughts and feelings.

rape Forced sexual acts.

rationalization Psychological coping mechanism in which you explain away something that has happened or is happening.

sexual violence Criminal behavior including rape, sexual assault, or violence or threats of violence to force a sexual act.

societal conditioning The way in which society and your community affect how you think and feel about yourself.

violation Broadly defined, includes physical violence, sexual violence, property crime, sexual harassment, unwanted touching, and emotional abuse.

Resource List

General Information

Gay Men's Health Crisis
129 West 20th Street
New York, NY 10011
212-337-3532
(For information on AIDS/HIV)

Planned Parenthood Federation of America
810 Seventh Avenue
New York, NY 10019
212-541-7800
(For information on birth control)

Planned Parenthood Federation of Canada
1 Nicholas Street, Suite 430
Ottawa, Ontario K1N 7B7
613-238-4474

Canadian Public Health Association
National AIDS Clearinghouse
1565 Carling Ave., Suite 400
Ottawa, Ontario K1Z 8R1
613-725-3769

Information on Crime and Victimization

Crime Victims Counseling
P.O. Box 023003
Brooklyn, NY 11202-0060
718-875-5862

National Victim Center
2111 Wilson Boulevard
Arlington, VA 22201
703-276-2880

60 In Canada, call 1-800-VICTIMS (1-800-842-8467)

Rape Crisis Centers (For a nationwide listing of rape crisis centers, call the Washington, DC, Rape Crisis Center Hotline, 202-333-7273, or check the phone book for local information)

Hospital Emergency Room
(Ask for Rape Trauma Center)

Ottawa Sexual Assault Support Centre Hotline
613-234-2266

Toronto Rape Crisis Centre Hotline
416-597-8808

The Police
(For emergencies, dial 911; check the phone book for local information)

Information on Self-Defense Training

Impact Personal Safety
19310 Ventura Boulevard
Tarzana, California 91356
818-757-3963

Prepare Self-Defense
25 West 43rd Street
New York, NY 10036
800-442-7273

Woman's Way Self Defense
512 Silver Spring Avenue
Silver Spring, MD 20910

The YWCA
(Check the phone book)

Martial Arts
(Check the phone book under Martial Arts or Karate)

In Canada, call Impact Personal Safety at 818-757-3963 for references to Canadian self-defense programs

For Further Reading

Bell, Ruth. *Changing Bodies, Changing Lives: A Book for Teens on Sex and Relationships.* New York: Random House, 1988.

Boston Women's Health Book Collective Staff. *The New Our Bodies, Ourselves.* New York: Simon and Schuster, 1992.

Brownmiller, Susan. *Against Our Will: Men, Women, and Rape,* rev.ed. New York: Bantam Books, 1988.

Caignon and Groves. *Her Wits About Her.* New York: Harper and Row, 1987.

Gilligan, Carol. *In a Different Voice: Psychological Theory and Women's Development.* Cambridge: Harvard University Press, 1982.

McCoy, Kathy, and Wibblesman, Charles. *The New Teenage Body Book,* rev.ed. Los Angeles: The Body Press, 1992.

Parrot, Andrea. *Coping with Date Rape and Acquaintance Rape,* rev.ed. New York: Rosen Publishing Group, 1995.

Wolf, Naomi. *The Beauty Myth.* New York: William Morris, 1991.

Index

63

Acknowledgments

This book is dedicated to Karen Chasen, the Executive Director at Prepare Self-Defense. Without her constant support, editorial eye, and sense of humor none of these books would have been completed. Many other people have taught me about self-defense and personal safety. Listing them all would take many pages. However, my deepest thanks go to Lisa Gaeta, Director of Impact Personal Safety, Los Angeles. Lastly, I want to thank my parents, who have always taught me to "be aware."

About the Author

Donna Chaiet, a practicing attorney in New York City, is the founder and President of Prepare, Inc. Prepare conducts personal safety programs that teach teenagers the verbal and physical skills required to defend themselves by training them to fight against a padded mock assailant. Ms. Chaiet is a recognized speaker and conducts safety/communication seminars for schools, community organizations, and Fortune 500 companies throughout the United States. Ms. Chaiet's frequent television appearances include CBS, NBC, ABC, WOR, FOX, Lifetime, Fox Cable, and New York 1.

Photo Credits

Cover, pp. 10, 18, 20, 23, 30, 37, 42, 48, 50, 55 by Michael Brandt; pp. 2, 18, 34 by Katherine Hsu; pp. 7, 15, 27 by Yung-Hee Chia; p. 24 by Lauren Piperno

Design

Kim Sonsky